26 Ways to Become a Better Manager

By

Kimberly Peters

For

26Ways.com

All Rights Reserved 2014 26ways.com

Other Books from 26 Ways. Com

26 Ways to Get More Fun from RC Aircraft

26 Ways to Manage Your Type 2 Diabetes

26 Ways to Save Money on your Utility Bills

26 Ways to Grow Your On-Line Business

Disclaimer

The materials in this book is designed to be used as a resource only and not to be considered a definitive action plan for any specific situation or individual. Since everyone is different and every situation is different, it is the responsibility of the reader to determine the suitability for any or all parts of this book as they pertain to their own situation. Neither the writers, distributors or publisher of this book assume any responsibility for the use or application of any or all parts of this book. This book may not be reproduced in any form without the express written permission of the author.

Contents

Introduction	5
Communicate Well	9
Listen Well	15
Value Others	23
Provide Feedback	27
Stay Calm	33
Have Common Sense	39
Have & Share a Vision	41
Delegate Responsibly	45
Setting Goals	50
Motivation	57
Learn from your Mistakes	62
Lead by Example	65
Grow Your Employees	68
Be Fair	72
Be Consistent	75
Be Confident	79
Be Reliable	84
Be Aware	87
Be Specific	91

Be Focused	94
Be a Team Player	98
Be Respectful	101
Be Organized	107
Be Reasonable	113
Be Able to Resolve Conflict	116
Be Human	120
Be Honest	124
Be Protective	126
Be an Isolationist	128
Conclusion	130

Introduction

There are many different types and levels of management in companies today and they all share a common purpose and goal. Their purpose is to take corporate directives or policies and make sure their employees follow them and get their work done. Their goal is to make the company better, larger and more profitable.

But the truth is a manager needs to accomplish much more than that in order to be a great manager who is well respected and who has a strong and lengthy track record of success. In order to achieve this ultimate goal of becoming a great manager, we must all broaden our ideas of what managers are and what they should become.

The facts are clear that when a manager is well respected and highly thought of that those under his leadership or on his or her team will work harder, longer and produce far better results. In other words, the purpose is not to become your employee's best friend but rather to have them believe that you are there for them as they are for you.

The best thing about becoming a great manager is that even though you are spending more of your time concentrating on your employees and their roles within the organization your workload actually becomes easier. You will find yourself with more time to dedicate to other important things on your plate because your employees require less overall attention and instruction.

A great manager also understands the need to be able to view certain things from multiple directions I order to provide the very best approach to accomplishing goals and achieving objectives. Once a manager is able to do this on a regular and daily basis, their teams achieve more in less time.

A great manager understands that there are more ways to measure success than in dollars and sense. They understand the value in employee contributions and they understand the need to develop employees so that they can see advancement in their futures as well.

This book is going to give you a lot of ways to help you make the transition from a good manager to a great one. While not every item in this book might pertain to you, they all will help you manage better and more efficiently and also help you get better results from your staff.

As you read through this book you might be skeptical about some of the suggestions and feel that a manager should not have to worry about something because you feel an employee should do that on their own without needing to be managed through it. But the reality is that many people DO need to be managed through a process in order to get the best results.

This is not a "touchy-feely" book about coddling employees and getting involved in their personal lives. Quite the contrary we cover what managers must do to create the very best work environment that makes employees WANT to perform better instead of needing to perform better. That is a huge difference and one that all great managers understand and subscribe to.

So go through this book with an open mind and pick out a few things that you think will work and a couple that you are skeptical about but willing to give a try. We are sure that once you get started, you will see the merit of every tip or chapter in this book and start going about implementing all of them.

Last, but certainly not least, if you feel that this is not worth all the effort, then let me appeal to your selfish side. The effort is not really all that much and when you do these things your life becomes easier. So that's a bonus for you. Second, great managers are in high demand so as you become a great manager you become more valuable and more valuable people earn higher salaries.

So if you are not willing to become a great manager for your employees and staff, become one for yourself. Because when you become a great manager everyone benefits.

Communicate Well

First and foremost, being a great manager, or even just an effective one, requires the ability to communicate your thoughts, ideas and intentions clearly and effectively. After all, you cannot expect someone to do what you tell them when you are unable to provide clear and easily understood instructions.

The communication process is not just talking loud enough for people to hear you. It involves both talking and listening, the proper choices of words, the tone and emotions behind those words as well as our body language and the environment in which we are communicating. If any of these factors are missing or weak, then the risk of being misunderstood grows much larger.

When it comes to management, we have an obligation to communicate with our employees or team members every day of the week. Whether it is to communicate instructions, ask questions, get clarification, give praise, critique performance or just to help carry on with normal business throughout the day, we need to know how to communicate effectively with everyone.

Everyone involved in a conversation or communication process must accept their part of the responsibility for understanding what is being communicated. Management cannot expect their messages to be received if their communication skills are weak or if their employees cannot or will not listen.

Likewise, an employee cannot expect to understand their part of the communication process if they are not paying attention or are distracted or just not capable of understanding what is being communicated. After all, people can only be expected to understand what they are able to understand.

From the previous two paragraphs we should easily be able to come to the understanding that good or proper communication is the responsibility of EVERYONE not just the one doing the talking. There MUST be a realization between everyone that each party must take total responsibility for understanding what is being communicated. There must not be any assessing of blame or excuses made because something the other person, or other people, have done or are doing.

From the managers point of view, they need to communicate in such a way that everyone who needs to understand will be able to understand them. That means talking clearly and loudly enough that people will be able to easily hear them when they speak.

If their words are mumbled or spoken so low that people have to strain to hear them, then the chances of people not hearing everything and then just "filling in the blanks" will decrease the overall accuracy of what is being communicated.

For example, if the manager is talking and people in the back row cannot hear him (or her), then the manager should be talking louder. But if no one speaks up and asks them to talk louder they are at fault as well. This is because there is an obligation on all parties to take whatever steps necessary so that everything is easy to understand.

The manager must speak clearly and with sufficient volume so that everyone can hear. They also must use words that are easily understood so there is no confusion or guesswork involved when it comes to understanding what was said. There is no room for fancy words that no one understands when it comes to effective communication.

The manager also needs to provide all the relevant information needed so people will know what they are saying and how to accomplish whatever it is that they are being asked to do. If people need to know 5 things in order to accomplish a task you are assigning them but you only give them information or explanations on three of those things, then there is bound to be trouble!

When it comes to communicating to a group of people with different levels of experience or expertise, the manager should always talk to the level of the least knowledgeable person.

This insures that everyone will understand and not just a few people. If there is just one person of extremely limited knowledge or experience then perhaps that person should be talked to by themselves or at least have another employee assigned to mentor them until they do become more knowledgeable.

A good manager will also take time out every so often to ask if there are any questions or to ask if everyone understood what they just talked about. This gives people a chance to get clarification on things they are not sure of before moving on and becoming even more confused. Communication works best when people can layer new information on a more solid base of existing knowledge.

A great manager also understands that nothing gets communicated well when it is difficult to concentrate or hear the conversation. This means choosing reasonably quiet and distraction free areas for important conversations. This means eliminating or reducing background noises so that they can be easily heard and also not having people distracted by constant phone calls or other interruptions.

Emotions can play a critical role in effective communication as well. Angry or upset people are not very good communicators. When people are angry their brains shut down, they jump to conclusions and they are far less receptive to new or different ideas.

With this in mind the manager should schedule meetings during the times of the day when people are the most relaxed and receptive to hearing what they have to say.

If an important conversation must take place and everyone is angry or upset, it might be worthwhile to put the conversation off until the next day or next week. A good manager understands that you cannot force someone to listen and comprehend. Just because the boss says so does not mean people can check their emotions at the door and listen effectively.

Another aspect of emotions and communication is that angry people sometimes say things they don't mean and often blow little things out of proportion because the anger inside them drives them to do so. Very little useful information comes out of communicating with an extremely angry person. A good manager will allow things to calm down first. If that is not possible a good manager will take steps to calm people down first before trying to start the communication process.

In the introduction we mentioned the need for the manager to be respected by his or her staff. This is important because if people respect each other they will tend to listen more and be more receptive to what is being discussed. People almost always have a more open mind when talking to people they respect.

But just because you are the manager does not mean that people MUST respect you. Respect is earned not demanded. You earn respect by your actions and behavior. Part of that behavior is perhaps one of the most important parts of the communication process for the manager. That part is listening and we will discuss that next.

Listen Well

Have you ever tried to carry on a conversation with someone who refuses to listen to what you are saying? Have you ever tried to get your point across when the other person constantly interrupts you or talks over you? Have you ever tried to communicate to someone else when they are talking on the phone or typing on their keyboard? Most of us run into these situations all the time both at work, at home and out in society. It just seems that people have forgotten how to listen anymore. And that's a shame.

Whenever someone does any of the above while you are talking to them or otherwise trying to communicate with them, it is like they are saying to you "I cannot be bothered with anything you have to tell me. I have other more important things to do with my time." Though they are not actually saying the words out loud, that is exactly what THEY are communicating to YOU!

In the role of the manager, it is critical that you take the time to listen to your employees or team members when they are talking to you. Do not adopt a superior position where their words mean nothing and yours are gospel even though that is what you might be thinking. It is all right to listen to opposing views and comments and then restate what you want to see happen. But never just cut someone off and dismiss their input without listening to it.

Listening is also important because when we listen we sometimes pick up little bits of information that we were not previously aware of. This can sometimes uncover flaws in our reasoning or approach and allow us to change our direction to avoid costly or embarrassing mistakes. Has we not listened we might never have received that information.

Whenever we interrupt someone from talking, we run the chance that we will never be told everything we need to make the right decisions or choices. By letting the person talk uninterrupted, we not only get more information but at the same time we are showing respect for the other person.

Listening also allows us to get different viewpoints of the same situation so we get some insight into how others might receive what we are trying to tell them. This might result in changing the words we use or maybe softening the approach so that people are not offended by what we are saying to them.

Getting other points of view is almost always useful to either confirm we are taking the right approach or making us aware of problems we never thought existed.

Even though we might be extremely intelligent and knowledgeable, there has not been a human being created so far that is always right or infallible. We all can learn from life experiences and learning how to listen makes that whole process a lot easier and faster.

Listening also enables us to calm people down so that the overall communication process goes easier and smoother. Just the act of listening to what an angry person has to say often results in much of the anger dissolving away as more and more words are spoken. By listening you are telling the other person that their feelings and problems are of interest to you and that you sincerely want to help them. Even if that is really not how you honestly feel, you are not conveying that to the other person.

Many people are surprised to discover that they really have no idea how to properly listen to something or someone in order to get all the relevant information that they need to make the right decisions and take the right actions. They either hear some of the information, just the beginning of the information or sometimes not any information at all. They hear the words but do not process their meaning.

Sometimes we hear part of the conversation and then think we know everything that is coming and tune out the rest of what's being said.

We are so consumed with figuring out what to do next and so sure we know what the real issue is, we feel we don't need any other information. Then, later when we find out things are not going as they should, we realize that we made the wrong decision because we did not have all the information.

A classic example of this is when a person has a problem and it initially appears that we already know what that problem is. When this occurs, our minds "fast forward" to what our actions are going to be. Then, we make a comments or suggest a resolution only to find that the person is angry because the problem is something totally different.

In these situations, we really need to let the other person talk all the way through the entire problem so we can get all the information we need to make the right decision or take the proper action. This means letting the person talk and also the asking of any questions we might have to allow us to get to the real cause without guesswork or assumption.

Another problem we frequently have is multi-tasking during the communication process. There are a lot of ways we can be distracted through trying to multi-tasking. Some examples might be typing a letter or e-mail during the conversation, surfing the web, answering e-mails, talking on the telephone, driving while talking and sometimes carrying on side conversations while someone else is talking.

We have all done every one of those things more than once in our lives. In fact, sometimes we are so busy we have no choice but to multi-task. But another unfortunate truth is that our brains cannot dedicate all its efforts on one thing when it is being asked to do two or three things. Brainpower is divided among all the tasks being done at any one time.

As a manager, try at all times to give your staff and others you full attention when carrying on a conversation with them. Not only will you be better able to fully understand what they are saying, but at the same time you are showing respect to the other people in the conversation.

Emotions are the emotional aspect of the conversation or communication. You would be surprised to realize how much we can learn from just listening to the emotions behind the words.

Emotions can help convey the seriousness of a situation or the anger and frustration that the other person might be feeling at the time of the conversation. Very often the emotional content of the conversation should influence our choice of wording or our overall reaction and response to the other person.

For example, if you "hear" the anger and frustration of someone who has had difficulty for a long time in getting resolution to a problem, you would be more receptive to getting personally involved rather than just telling that person who to contact to get some action taken. This would be because the other person already tried that and did not get the proper response.

Closely tied to emotions are the physical manifestations of our emotions. This is usually referred to as "body language". Body language is how we present ourselves physically during the communication process. Our stance might be very aggressive or even confrontational or we might appear relaxed and laid back. But regardless how we appear, our emotional state at that time will show through is our physical presence.

Understanding body language is important because not only do we have to "read" the other person's body language we also have to be aware of what our body language is as well. A relaxed presence might tend to diffuse anger and calm a person down while an aggressive or confrontational stance might inflame things and escalate the situation.

Though this may surprise most of you, the actual words we use are less than15% of the entire communication process. Even though words are important, the emotions behind them, the way we say them and how we present ourselves at the time make up far more of the overall communication content.

As managers, we need to be aware of all these things so not only do we communicate the proper message word wise but also in the way we look and act at the same time. We need to take note of our body language and deliver the appearance and perception that we are always in control and confident in our skills and abilities.

This is not something that comes naturally to some people and even more people might never be aware that how we look and how we present ourselves via our body image plays such a large role in the communication process.

Employees and Team Members want a manager who is calm and confident even in the most stressful situations. This all comes out in the way we communicate to others and how well we communicate our thoughts, ideas and instructions. We cannot expect people to do what we ask when we are unable to communicate it to them in a clear and easy to understand manner.

A good rule of thumb is to always ask at the end of the conversation or presentation if there are any questions or if there was anything that was not made clear. This will give people an easy chance to ask questions and to clear up any misunderstandings they currently might have.

Asking for questions is also useful to the manager because it gives the manager feedback on how well they communicated things to their staff. If everything goes well and there are few questions, it can be assumed that you communicated things very well. But if there are a lot of questions, a lot of confusion and a bunch of mistakes, that is an indication that the overall communication process has failed at some point.

Good and effective communication makes everyone's life easier and help us reduce errors and mistakes and drastically reduces wasted time and resources. Though effective communication takes some effort and possibly a bit more time, in the long run it saves time and resources because it eliminates wasted time and efforts.

Value Others

Good managers value their employees, co-workers, superiors and everyone else involved in their business and processes. Several things happen when you value other people. We become more responsive, more respectful and overall more engaged with those people, their needs and their contributions to the company.

Throughout my career I have seen managers who feel they are above everyone else and that others are just there to serve them and do their bidding. While that may very well be true in certain situations, the fact that their employees felt marginalized by that attitude resulted in everyone being less productive, less receptive and less satisfied in their jobs.

Good managers recognize the efforts and contributions of the people that work with them and under them. They realize that the overall success of the department or team is a result of the combination of the efforts of everyone not just one or two people.

They realize when everyone works together towards achieving a common goal that productivity goes way up.

Valuing others also means giving recognition and credit when and where it is due. It means not taking credit for the work done by others and giving deserving employees or team members the recognition they deserve.

Everyone likes to be acknowledged for the contributions they make and they feel good when this actually happens.

But some managers like to take the credit for everything their department or teams do. They take all the credit and accolades and don't let any of that credit filter down to the people actually responsible for the work that was done. When people see others take credit for their work, they feel under-valued, under-appreciated and not an important or vital part of the company.

As a great manager, we need to take things to another whole level. We need to make sure that our employees understand that their manager not only appreciates what they do but also understand how valuable they are to the overall process.

This is important because sometimes certain employees are so removed from the end result that they never see the fruits of their labors or the results their work produced. Because of this they never understand the value in what they are doing and lack of motivation sometimes is the result.

People need to have a purpose in what they do. They need to see the value in doing what they do and they need to be made aware of the end result of their labors.

We cannot assume that people know they are valued, we must show them. We need to recognize them for the work they do and the quality they represent.

When people think of recognition they usually think of money. While money is nice, it is not a particularly good long term motivator. Money works when you first get it, but after a while, it lacks the same motivational force. Instead, people like to get a pat on the back, a few nice words once in a while and the feeling they get because they know they are doing a good job.

People also perform at a much higher level when they feel respected and valued as employees. Almost everyone takes pride in doing a good job. But pride comes out of knowing you are doing well and the only way to get that feeling is through recognition, praise and knowing that your work is valued by the company.

This doesn't take much effort. A great manager does not assume the employees know they are valued, they make SURE they know they're valued.

They create a culture where all employees know they are part of a team and that they are all valued and respected. They give praise when warranted and they give encouraging words when appropriate.

But even more important, great managers often do one little thing on a regular basis that makes most employees put a smile on their faces. It takes just a couple of seconds but the effect can linger on for a long time.

It's really easy, doesn't cost you or the company any money and can be done at any time for any reason. Try it and see how it works. What is this little easy to do thing?

Just tell your people "Thank you!"

Try it because it works!

Provide Feedback

One of the most common complaints from workers in all type of jobs is that they never get any type of feedback on how well they are doing at their job. They keep working and trying hard but never discover whether what they are doing is good, bad or somewhere in between. When this happens, workers get frustrated and sometimes disillusioned.

Most employees want to do a good job. They want to do well for several reasons. It might just be so they keep their job or maybe they are looking to move up in the company. Maybe they are looking to get experience to move on with another company. Whatever the reason might be, most people, if given the chance, would prefer to do a good job instead of a bad job.

Sometimes you might have ways of judging your performance.

A sales person, for example, might look at their overall sales numbers and if they are where they are supposed to be then one might assume they were doing a good job. If they were really down, that might be an indication that you were not doing a great job.

This is true for any job that is measured by numbers or measureable criteria. But a lot of jobs might not be directly measurable or not measureable at the employee or individual level. In these kinds of positions, the only way an individual can really know whether or not they are doing a good job is by the commentary and feedback for their supervisor, manager or co-workers.

When people go to work each day and work hard but have no idea if they are doing a good job or not, they eventually become frustrated because they are putting out all their efforts, and spending all their time, and they don't know if any of their efforts are good enough or not. This is almost always because they have received no feedback from their manager.

Think about how you would feel if you worked very hard on something but never knew if you were doing a good job or if the final product or result was well received or not. Eventually you would just either give up or do enough just to exist because you know nothing else.

A great manager takes the time to formally go over every employee's performance at least once a year and informally several more times than that over the course of the year. This allows the employee the ability to know what they are doing well and what they need to do differently or improve upon. This allows the employee a chance to understand their performance level and make the changes they need to succeed.

Other than the formal evaluation, a good manager will take the time to stop and tell an employee when they have done a good job or whenever the results of something already completed were very well received. This kind of "pat on the back" can go a long way towards making an employee feel needed, appreciated and valued. It also lets them know that what they are doing is good and that they should continue along those lines.

When feedback is missing or absent, a few things can occur. People who are doing a good job might not think they are and change something that actually makes them do a worse job. They do this not because they know they are doing something wrong but just because they think they are doing something wrong.

On the other hand, someone doing a poor job because their approach or methodology was wrong may never realize their errors and keep on doing the same thing because they honestly believe they are doing a good job. So they never get the ability to change because they are not aware that change is needed.

There are also two kinds of feedback and a good manager knows how to handle each type. The two types we are referring to are positive feedback when a person does something right and negative feedback which happens whenever someone does something wrong or not up to standards. Each type of feedback should be handled in a different way.

Positive feedback can be handled in private or in a group setting or both. A good manager might meet with the employee in a private setting to give the pat on the back but then also recognize the good effort in front of the group. Most employees like the recognition and the mention in front of their co-workers and peers. It makes people feel good to have their efforts publically acknowledged.

Negative feedback, on the other hand, should always be handled individually and in private. The only exception might be if an entire team did a poor effort and the manager wants to teach the team how to do a better job next time. As long as no one member was the cause of the poor effort, a group discussion might work.

But when one person does something wrong or performs at a low level, the manager should always discuss this with the employee privately.

This was no one else is aware and the employee does not feel embarrassed or awkward. The manager can then instruct the employee on how they can do better in the future and provide guidance. In some cases, the employee can be placed on an improvement plan if such a plan is warranted.

A good manager understands that not only is feedback a good idea but it is also a necessary process. Contrary to popular belief our employees want to know how they are doing and want to know when they are doing something wrong or when their quality of work is not where it should be. It is when employees have no idea whether they are performing well or poorly that frustration creeps in.

I had a manager once who bragged that he never told an employee when he thought they were overloaded or doing a good job because he wanted them to always feel insecure so they would push themselves harder and harder. It was his opinion that he would get more productivity out of a scared and insecure employee than he would out of a confident and secure employee. It turns out he was dead wrong.

Not only didn't he get more out of his employees but he had one of the highest employee turnover rates in the country. It was because instead of trying harder employees started to feel frustrated and underappreciated and instead of trying harder, they spent more of their efforts on finding new employment.

Once a new job came along, they were gone! So much for his approach to employee relations.

This is one example of why great managers make it a priority to interact with their employees and give them feedback, instruction and encouragement on a regular basis. They do this not because they have to but because they want to. They see the value in keeping their employees motivated and fulfilled at work. Providing feedback on individual performance is one way of accomplishing this.

Stay Calm

Good managers understand the need to create an image and perception that they are always in control and never overwhelmed no matter how bad or hectic situations might get. This is important because when the manager appears in control, the employees feel that they have someone who can lead them through any crisis or situation. No one feels scared because the boss or manager has everything under control.

The vast majority of the time, especially in larger companies, the employees are not always aware of everything that is going on. So they have no way of understanding what is happening or why. To make matters even worse, sometimes rumors circulate containing false, or at least inaccurate information that makes matter worse. When this happens, they look towards the manager for reassuring and to regain confidence. This is just human nature.

Also, there will be times when deadlines are rapidly approaching or when a large project or assignment comes through with a seemingly impossible deadline. Or it could be any situation that causes stress among the employees. These are also times when they look to the manager for clarification and reassurance.

A good manager will be proactive in these situations and already have a plan in action that will address it. Or, at the very least, he will know how to go about creating the plan and then put that plan in action. Regardless of what may transpire, the great manager always appears in control and never nervous, overwhelmed or upset.

This is not to say that the manager doesn't really feel that way. He or she might be scared to death or have absolutely no clue about what to do or how to proceed. After all, just because you are a manager does not mean you have all the answers. In fact, the real answer might be that something really is overwhelming. But in front of the employees, the manager should always attempt to appear in control.

Sometimes this might mean closing the doors to your office and just think for a while to determine what can be done to make the situation appear easier or more organized. Perhaps the manager can borrow resources or knows how to involve outside resources or additional resources that will make the entire situation easier and better for everyone concerned.

In other words, the manager doesn't have to know all the answers but he should know how to start going about getting them. A good manager appears calm and tackles things one at a time instead of taking on a huge problem all by himself or all at once. A good manager will break down huge tasks to make them appear easier and more manageable. Never is this skill more important than when the manager has to relay news of a large upcoming project or assignment.

By taking a huge project or assignment and breaking it down into little pieces and assigning those pieces out to the team, the impact on everyone is reduced and the employees will see how if everyone works together that they can accomplish everything well within the established goal. With this message everyone sees the workload divided equally among the team and that the manager has everything well planned out.

A good manager understands that some employees can get overwhelmed very easily when confronted with a large project or assignment. So rather than induce a panic or over reaction when he makes his presentation, he can soften the impact by giving his or her own plan for accomplishing the goal or completing the project. And he can introduce all of this is a calm and professional manner.

Calm management provides security and belief among employees. If they see the manager isn't overwhelmed by whatever is going on they will tend to be calmer as well. But if the manager panics, everyone else will soon panic as well. Think of the captain on a sinking ship. If he remains calm and keeps the passengers calm, they will get everyone into the lifeboats and to safety. But when the captain panics and the passengers stampede. Not everyone makes it to safety.

The effective manager will look at something and figure the best way to introduce this to his or her staff. They will present it in the most positive way possible and also present it in such a way that the perceived impact to everyone is lessened. This is a far better approach than just telling people what has to be done and that everyone will just have to buckle down and do it.

Last but certainly not least, there will be times when bad things are going to happen and there is nothing that can be done about it. It might mean longer hours for everyone or it might mean a segment of the work force will be losing their jobs because of a dip in sales. During these bad times, the employees are going to look to the manager to make sense out of what is happening and how everyone is going to get through the tough times ahead.

During these times, the manager must remain calm even when he knows it is going to be really bad in the near future. The manager should not show fear or nervousness or give the impression that he or she feels there is no way everyone is going to get through this. The manager must deal with reality but he can also take steps to protect his or her employees during the tough times.

Though we will talk about this more in depth later on, one of the most important parts of management is isolating the really bad or concerning matters from those employees who have no control over those things. This means not spreading rumors, reassuring those employees that you know will not be effected by what is happening while helping everyone else through the transition.

In other words, the manager must always be the strong presence in the office that people can turn to for security and reassurance. The manager is also the person people can turn to with their questions and have enough faith in that they will believe that things will turn out all right.

Are things always going to turn out right? Of course not. Life is full of negative experiences and things that don't quite go the way we intended or wanted them to go. But it is how we react to those situations that helps shape how well we cope with these situations. If we remain calm, those around us will remain calm as well.

People who don't panic tend to be more productive. Productive people and productive minds are what is needed to lift ourselves out of difficult situations. It is only when we allow panic to take over does it become much harder to make it through. Great managers understand this and also understand their need to present a calm and strong appearance to all of their employees.

Have Common Sense

Some managers do things or expect things that just drive people crazy. While many times employees just don't understand because they do not have all the information or circumstances surrounding the request, many times it just appears the request or comments just make no sense at all.

Some managers like to create "busy work" or just do things because they are the boss and they are able to make employees do those things. For these types of managers these requests are just power based and most of the time employees resent them.

Other managers want what they want because that is what they need to have happen in order to meet a request from their bosses. It might not make any sense to your manager either but since he has been given his or her marching orders they are just passed down for you to deal with.

Regardless of the reasons, every manager needs to manage with a certain degree of common sense. This means being aware of what you are demanding or expecting and making sure it is doable or achievable. For example, you would not tell an employee that they have an hour to do a report that normally requires 3 days to complete.

Employees crave stability and confidence in their bosses and managers. This means understanding that there are valid reasons for everything they do. When a manager fails to use common sense in their instructions or commands, they lose credibility with their employees.

Have & Share a Vision

Great managers are visionaries. By that we mean that they can look into the future and see how what we do today will impact us and the company tomorrow. This is an important skills because much of what employees do every day is geared towards establishing and growing business in the future.

Management is tasked with making sure the company not only exists tomorrow but thrives and grows as well. This means taking the necessary steps today to insure growth and prosperity in the future.

Sometimes this means developing new products, seeking out another part of the marketplace, perhaps an acquisition or two and several other things that businesses and companies of all shapes and sizes to help keep their products and services current and fresh.

Sometimes the problem is that our employees are not aware of how what they are being asked to do today will impact the company tomorrow. They might see little benefit or question why this has to be done and done now. This is especially true when the assignment or task is a total departure from what the company is doing now.

Employees are not aware of what the future holds for them and they are not aware of how the company intends to operate and remain in business. A great manager makes their employees aware of what is going on now and what plans are for the future. They will explain what the direction of the company is and why they are taking that particular approach.

While employees do not need to know every single detail, they do need to understand where the company stands now and where it is planning to be in the future. This is especially true in areas where things change rapidly. Big companies don't plan just for next week or next month. They plan years in advance so that they are always having projects in the works to carry them through changes in the marketplace.

It is up to the manager to communicate all of this to their employees.

This can help reduce fears, gives the employees confidence that the company is going to still be around in the future and that management has the knowledge and ability to properly lead the company in the right direction.

There will also be times when the manager needs to show his or her own personal vision for not only the company but for their own department. This can create excitement within the employees as they begin to see a new purpose or direction for the department. If this vision includes growth and opportunities for the employees, this can create a very positive outlook for the future as well.

Most employees want to feel that they are involved in the future of the company. They want to feel that they are part of the team and part of the changes and growth within the company. By making every employee aware of what the future holds for them and the company you are letting them into the process and making them part of it.

Employees also want to know that their own future is safe and secure. Uncertainty is a reason a lot of people leave jobs they love in order to find employment they feel is more secure. By sharing your vision and the company's vision for the future, you are creating a feeling of confidence and security in the minds of the employees.

This will reassure each employee and reduce the number of employees who will seek more stable employment elsewhere.

Naturally, if the future holds something really bad or a bleak outlook, you have a choice to make. You can choose not to share that particular information until the right point in time so you do not cause stress in the workplace or you can share it and be right out in front of it. That approach at least gives your employees knowledge of what lies ahead and what the plans are to deal with whatever is going on.

If rumors are out there, or if people see a change in the marketplace that appears to affect your company, it is almost always better for the manager to develop a plan for dealing with it and get that plan out to their employees as quickly as possible. Share the plan with as positive a view as possible but keep it factual.

Never lie or mislead your employees because when a manager does that, they lose the credibility and the trust of the employees. When that happens it is very had to reestablish that trust and sometimes it never fully returns. Work with management to decide on how to release the information in the best way possible to make sure your employees feel part of the process and are not blindsided by the problems when they occur.

Delegate Responsibly

Part of every manager's responsibilities involve delegation of tasks and responsibilities. This helps ensure that everything gets done in an organized manner without overburdening any one or two people within the office. This is required because it is usually impossible for one person to handle all the responsibilities in the department or office. So, to avoid confusion and to make sure everything is handled properly and fairly it is up to the manager to determine who does what.

Usually delegation is based on individual skills and abilities as well as experience and workload. The result is that each task is being handled by the people best suited for that particular task. This results in higher productivity and better overall results.

It just makes sense for the person with the graphics background to be assigned graphics projects and the person with the writing talents be assigned the copy writing or other responsibilities.

Using the people with the right talents for the right job just makes more sense. Tasks get done in less time with better results when they are properly assigned.

Another reason for delegation is speed. It makes sense that when one person tries to do everything that only one thing gets done at a time. Even when one person tries to do 3 things at once each task takes longer. So delegating 5 tasks to 5 different people means that all 5 of those tasks are being handled at the same time! This saves a ton of time and helps the team meet even tough deadlines.

But sometimes delegation is done using other criteria and rational which might not be appreciated by some people within the office. When this happen, the end result is stress and tension within the office.

For example, I once had a job where my boss was always asking me to be on task forces, handle projects and head up groups to accomplish certain tasks. While I always accepted these assignments without complaint, I began to realize that I was doing the lion's share of the work while others weren't being asked to do much of anything. Naturally I questioned this because I didn't feel it was fair. The response I received back was that I was being asked because my boss knew if I did something it would always be done right and without problems. When others were assigned tasks problems always arose. So most of everything was assigned to me.

Now while I was flattered and pleased that my manager thought so highly of me, I was also a little annoyed that I was working so much harder, and sometimes longer, than most everyone else. In fact, there were two of us doing the lion's share of the work while other sat back and watched. It is nice to be appreciated but it is not nice to be abused or overworked.

In this example the manager is delegating in such a way that the distribution of work was done in an unfair manner where some people were given more or less work than others. The result was that people were rewarded for doing poor quality work by never being asked to do anything ever again. The people who did quality work were, in fact, penalized by being given a higher volume of work than other employees without receiving additional compensation.

Another common example would be a manager who likes some employees, or even a single employee, better than the other employees and delegates work based on those friendships. For example the manager gives his "friend" all the nice or easy assignments while others get the nasty assignments. Though this certainly isn't fair, it is a fairly common situation in many offices.

A good manager will delegate tasks strictly by who is best qualified to do the work and then who has the lowest workload. If the only qualified person has the highest workload then the good manager will off load some of that workload to someone else thus freeing the time necessary to do the new assignment.

If certain people do poor quality of work they should be told that they need to start producing higher quality work or risk disciplinary action. They should not simply be given a pass because of their poor skills or work habits. When this happens they are getting rewarded for doing subpar work.

Another way a good boss can delegate is by asking people to volunteer for some assignments and then assign the work accordingly. This can result in people getting more of the work they enjoy and are good at. In this approach the manager needs to keep records of who volunteered for what assignment because there will always be people who never volunteer for anything.

If someone does volunteer for an extra assignment the manager can also say, "OK, now that Alice is going to undertake the Zimmerman Project, we will need someone to take over some of her existing responsibilities. Dan, you can take over XXXX and Lou, you can do ZZZZ until Alice is finished with the project."

This sends a few messages. First, it shows the manager is aware of individual workloads and is interested in not overburdening any one employee. Second, it also lets people know if they don't volunteer they might be chosen for reassignment of other work. This sends a message that laziness is not going to be tolerated.

This is important because you cannot just let people figure out who is going to do what. There will always be people who will try to do the least amount of work possible and those people will hide from tasks as long as they can get away with it.

From the manager's point of view, delegation is necessary because no manager can be expected to handle everything for everyone. A good manager understands this and delegates important tasks to others so everything can be handled properly by those with the skills and abilities necessary to accomplish those tasks.

Plus, the responsibility for getting everything done lies with the manager. The manager is the one charged with the deadline and it is up to the manager to use the resources he or she has in the best and most efficient way possible so those deadlines can be met. If those deadlines are not met it is the manager who takes the fall. If they are met the managers takes the credit. So it just makes sense that it is the responsibility of the manager to assign or delegate work to the people they think are best suited for it.

Setting Goals

Good managers understand the need for goals and the power behind them. Contrary to what most people might believe, employees actually like to have some kind of established goals. Goals allow us a way to gauge how well we are doing in our jobs and how well we are performing. This kind of feedback helps keep people engaged and aware of their own individual performance. Goals are also useful by establishing specific criteria against which all employees are measured equally and fairly.

But in order for goals to be useful and to have them be a positive influence, goals must adhere to certain parameter and characteristics. The most common way people usually refer to quality goals is to use the S.M.A.R.T. goal acronym. Now let's discuss what each letter in that acronym refers to.

Specific

In order to be effective, goals need to be specific so everyone understands exactly what needs to be done or accomplished.

The more a goal is defined and the less ambiguity in the goal the more effective it becomes.

Which goal do you think will be better? "Improve sales next year" or "Improve Sales by 17% by year end".

The first goal is very vague and technically if you sold $100,000 worth or product last year and this year you sold $100,001 you would have hit your goal even though you only sold $1 more this year. So I'm sure you can see the fault with this goal.

When creating a goal, be as specific as you need to be so that everyone understands EXACTLY what you are looking for. Kind of understanding means it was not specific enough for at least some people. Make it specific, word it clearly and avoid confusion.

Measureable

The second factor in a good goal is that it has to be able to be measured by concrete methods of measurement. In other words, it cannot be measured by anything objective or based on opinion or judgment.

Which goal do you think is better? "Do better this year" or "Increase the number or orders processed each month by 10%?

The first goal is almost totally objective. How on earth would you measure whether someone did better this year? Did that mean sell more, work longer, and work harder or more efficiently?

I mean how would you decide if someone did better? One person might think someone did better and someone else might think they did worse. This is because this particular goal is all objective.

The second goal is better because it shows you exactly what needs to be improved upon and how much improvement is desired. Now the employee knows exactly what to concentrate their efforts on. Reports can be used to clearly show the amount of improvement. Either the employee processed 10% more orders or they didn't. Figures are not subjective so you can compare person to person fairly and equally.

Achievable

Here is where a lot of managers and companies go wrong. In order for a goal to be motivating and positive, it MUST be achievable! If you give someone a goal that is so unrealistic that it could never be achieved then it ceases to be a positive influence on the employee. Instead, the employee either gets frustrated or stops trying, or they just outright dismiss the goal as being totally BS and stop trying. Either way the end result is not a positive one.

For example, let's say you are a salesman and your boss tell you that he wants to see a 10% increase in sales next year.

That might be achievable depending on the industry and situation. So you look at the goal and start trying to find ways to reach that goal. You might create a new sales pitch or seek out another segment of the market in order to raise sales. But no matter what you try, you are at least trying to hit that goal because you feel that it is attainable.

But let's say your manager sits down with you and tells you he wants to see a 12,000% improvement in sales next year! What would your reaction be then? Would you try as hard? Probably not. Would you be angry and frustrated because you were being set up to fail? Probably. Would you view this goal as a positive or negative part of your job? Probably a negative one. In order for goals to work as a positive reinforcement, they MUST be achievable!

Now it is perfectly fine to want to push your employees a little bit if you think they are capable. In those situations a good manager might create two goals. One is the regular goal and the second are a set of "stretch goals" which are higher or more difficult to achieve but are still achievable under the right circumstances.

Using the example above, the regular goal was a 10% improvement in sales while the stretch goal might be a 15% improvement. This way the employee will try hard to hit their regular goals and also try hard to reach their stretch goals. Not hitting a stretch goals would not be considered a negative for the employee though. Stretch goals work well when there is a reward for hitting them.

Realistic

Though similar to the achievable factor, goals must also be realistic under normal conditions. For example, our previous example of a 10% increase might be achievable but if the full goal was "achieve a 10% increase in sales within one hour" then that goal would not be realistic.

The chief rule of thumb is when all the parameters of the goal are determined the overall goal must be realistic in nature. That means the time frame and size of the goal, along with the circumstances surrounding that goal must be realistic.

For example, that 10% increase in sales might be realistic if you are in a growing market. But if your products are outdated or otherwise have been in a sales decline over the last 5 years, it would not be realistic to expect a 10% increase all of a sudden unless there was an expected change of the products or the marketplace.

A good manager understands the employee, the marketplace and the company itself when assigning goals. He will also determine if the employee actually has control over most of what is entailed in that particular goal to make sure the goals are realistic and fair to the employee.

Timely

Every goal needs to be assigned a time frame.

It has been said that the difference between a goal and an objective is just a date. Taking over the lead in market share is an objective. Taking over the lead in market share by the end of December is a goal.

People need goals with clearly stated time frames because it lets them know how much time they have to reach that certain goal. Without a time frame goals become muddy and confusing. If I give you a 10% increase in sales as a goal and you bring in a big order the first week, does that mean you achieved your goal even though sales are flat for the rest of the year? It could because no time frame was stated in the goal. So that is subject to interpretation.

So when creating goals make sure you include a time frame for every goal and that the time frame is reasonable, fair and appropriate for that particular goal. Time frames must be created with common sense in mind. Asking people to achieve too much in too short of a time frame leads to frustration and anger.

A good manager also understands that there can always be too much of a good thing and that goals and goal setting are no exception. A few critical and well placed goals can be a great thing to provide feedback and evaluation for both individuals and teams of employees. But if you create too many goals, then problems often occur.

I once worked in a position where we started having goals. At first there were 4 basic goals and that was good because it gave us all something to focus upon in our jobs.

Nobody minded those 4 goals and they achieved their purpose very nicely.

But the next year we had 8 goals followed by 14 the year after. Somewhere between those 8 and 14 goals most of the employees lost focus. Certain goals were opposite with one another which meant that if you worked to achieve one you hurt your chances of achieving another. It finally got to the point that most employees just ignored the goals and just tried to do a good job. In that case, too many goals were counter-productive.

The good manager also understands that sometimes things outside of anyone's control can have a profound impact on someone's ability to achieve their goals. For example, if the economy takes a nose dive and stocks fail, people might not purchase much of your product because they are concerned about their money and future. Or, if your warehouse burns to the ground and it takes 6 months to restock it with product, your sales are bound to suffer. Again, this is not under anyone's control.

So the great manager needs to know how to create reasonable, accurate and specific goals. They also need to make those goals achievable as well. Then the manager must be able to look at those goals and realize and understand the factors surrounding those goals so he or she can draw the right conclusions based on every part of the situation and not just the hard facts.

Motivation

In simple terms, a good manager is also a good motivator. Good managers provide an environment where every employee is encouraged to do their best work and receives recognition for doing so. Motivation helps keep employees engaged and performing at a higher level.

Good managers understand the value of keeping people properly motivated and the various ways of doing so. Whether it is by constant encouragement, rewarding top performers, assigning goals or through any other method, good managers motivate their employees to better themselves and perform at consistently higher levels.

Good managers also understand that not everyone responds the same way to the same forms of motivation. For some money is the prime motivator while for others it might be recognition that is most important. Other employees might value having a challenge at work and prefer not to become bored or remain stagnant at work.

The good manager will find the best approach for every employee and use that to keep every employee motivated and engaged.

Good managers also understand that some forms of motivation are not really motivators at all and do not use them. For example, fear is not a good motivator. Those who manage through fear and coercion not only do not motivate their employees, they anger them into looking for employment elsewhere.

At one job I held (for a short time) general manager used to motivate through fear. He would fire their service manager and sales manager every 6 months to send a message to others that they better perform or they were out of a job. Not only didn't this motivate the employees, it made the General Manager a laughingstock. No one took him seriously and no one bothered to work hard at much of anything other than looking for another job. Employee turnover was sky high, good people left to work at competitors and eventually the company went out of business!

It never ceases to amaze me what some people call motivation. Telling someone they should be happy to still have a job is not motivating. Telling people if they don't perform there are other people waiting who will perform is not motivating. Telling people they are worthless and that they better shape up or lose their job is not motivating!

Curiously, money is not a long term motivator either. Though commissions might be motivators because the more people sell the more they earn, salary increases are short-term motivators at best. Think about that for a minute. Remember the last time you asked for a raise and got it? The money looked great in the first few checks but after a while you got used to it and it ceased to motivate you. The problems and situations that existed before you received the raise are still there.

What does motivate employees? Well the fact is most of what motivates people always comes back to a sense of appreciation and belonging. Money equates to an employee's value to the company. Praise and a good word every now and then equates to showing appreciation. Even something as simple as showing concern and listening to employees make them feel more valuable and a more important part of the company.

Proper motivation makes employees WANT to do more or do things better. In other words they do things because they want to and not because they have to. Good managers will constantly provide motivation to every employee. That motivation might be in terms of contests or bonuses, maybe giving hard workers who do a great job a day off or a gift certificate to take their spouse out to dinner or something like that.

It is not so much the size of the gesture as it is the gesture itself. But even that might have its limits.

Motivation only exists when the other person, or other people, see the value of what is involved as being appropriate. For example, if you want to thank someone for doing a great job and working hard and their reward is a $5 gift certificate to a fast food restaurant, that might be view as insulting or condescending. But if on a Friday you hand out that same $5 certificate right before lunch and just tell everyone to go out and enjoy a treat on you that would be viewed as a positive gesture. It is all in the context in which the gesture is given.

A good manager will be on the lookout for ways to motivate their employees. Motivation should not be something that happens once a year or only during special times of the year. In order to be most effective, motivation must be on-going. It must be constant and people should always be encouraged to better themselves. Employees should also be encouraged to improve their skills and congratulated when they do so.

Another extremely effective method of motivation is to provide opportunities for advancement to those who do better themselves and improve their performance. When companies promote qualified people from within it motivates people to do better and do more. That is because there is an incentive for doing so.

But if a company always brings in people from outside the organization to fill higher spots in the company, that tells the employees there is no reason to make yourself better because there is no advancement for you. A good manager will look closely at their employees to fill better or higher positions first before looking outside the company.

Company picnics, social activities after work and other forms of recreational activities also help provide a sense of camaraderie and can get workers to work more closely together. In addition these events are another way of the company telling everyone that they appreciate their efforts and hard work.

Whatever the method and whenever it occurs, the great manager understands how important it is to properly and positively motivate every employee. When this happens everything gets better. People grow into better roles, performance goes up and people are just happier overall at work.

Learn from your Mistakes

No matter how smart we are, how much education we have or how hard we try, no one is perfect. We all make mistakes and it is what we do after making the mistakes that makes all the difference in the world. This is especially true when it comes to the manager.

No employee expects the manager to be perfect and no is shocked when mistakes happen. But what they look for in a manager is someone who takes responsibility for their actions, stands behind their employees and most important, someone who learns from their mistakes.

Making mistakes is one of the most powerful learning processes we have in life. We can read something in a book or from hearing someone speak at a seminar but until we actually try it, and sometimes fail, we never truly "learn" it. But in order for mistakes to be positive in nature, we need to take responsibility for them, acknowledge them and understand why a particular mistake was the wrong thing to do so we can stop from doing that again in the future.

For the manager this is a two-edged sword. When a manager makes a mistake they need to take responsibility for it and learn from the experience so they don't do it again. This, as we just said, is part of the learning experience. As long as we learn from our mistakes and stop from doing them over and over and over again, the net result can be viewed as a positive.

But the same holds true for an employee as well. If an employee makes an honest mistake, the manager should not come down with massive punishments or terminate the employee for making that mistake. Instead, they should make certain that the employee knows what they did wrong, understands the impact the mistake made and then does not make the same mistake again in the same situation.

So as the manager wants to be forgiven for their mistakes, so must the manager forgive the mistakes of their employees. But if the manager or employee makes the same mistakes over and over again, that is something else.

Sometimes mistakes can be used as teaching points to help other perform higher, better and with more accuracy and fewer mistakes. The thing about mistakes is that if one person makes a particular mistake, others might make the same mistake as well. By using one person's mistake as a teaching point, everyone can learn to avoid those same mistakes in the future.

Of course, when using mistakes as teaching points, it is not necessary, or advisable, to share who made that mistake in the first place.

That would just embarrass the person who made the mistake and place a negative on the teaching aspect of the situation. Just point out the mistake, leaving the person who made it a mystery, point out why it was wrong and move on. Making anyone embarrassed or upset does no one any good.

A great manager will establish an environment where people will try hard not to make mistakes but at the same time will not be afraid to try new things or make decisions when needed. This is not always an easy environment to create but a great manager understands the value in creating such an environment.

So when you make a mistake, own up to it, take responsibility for it and most important, learn from it. Also, introduce this same process and culture into the work environment so employees can function at a higher level and also learn from their mistakes.

Lead by Example

Like it or not, many employees look up to their managers or at least look to them for guidance and support. This is a vital aspect of the relationship between a manager and the employee and it is the responsibility for the manager to exhibit the kind of behavior and action that they wish to see from employees. After all, you cannot act one way and expect others to behave differently.

Great managers are careful in what they do and how they do it. They model the behavior that they desire everyone else to model. They interact with others in a proper and efficient manner and they go about doing their job at a high level or performance. IN other words, a great manager serves as a role model for their employees.

For example, if the manager strolls in 30 minutes late and walks out an hour early, that does not set a good example for the rest of the staff. The manager cannot expect other employees to work hard, arrive early and leave late because that is what is needed to properly do their jobs or achieve a deadline.

Instead, the manager should arrive early and stay later to set the proper example for their employees.

If the manager walks around and tells inappropriate jokes or is disrespectful to the employees, chances are that type of behavior is going to spread within the workplace. The same goes for quality of work, respect for others and even personal appearance. After all, if the boss comes to work in jeans and a T-shirt, he would have a difficult time disciplining others for violating the company dress code!

Many people are hesitant to ask for guidance or be given instruction on the proper way to so things. They are hesitant because they feel that this might make them look stupid or less competent in the eyes of others. People who feel this way often look to others, either co-workers or their manager, for indication on how to do something the right way.

By going about your work in the right manner, the manager can set a level of expectation that is higher than it normally might be and they can do this without saying a word. When the manager is thorough and never cuts corners it is more likely that their staff will take that approach as well. But if the manager is lazy and always looks for the easy way out, their employees are likely to pick up some of those bad habits as well.

When it comes to being a great manager, perception is one of the most important keys in how a manager is perceived by the employees. As we have already stated, employees are not looking for perfection in their manager. They are looking for guidance, security and for someone that they can rely on when they have problems or issues. They want someone that can have faith in to do the right thing and to look up to when they need it.

If their manager is someone who always tries to do the right thing in the right way then the employees will tend to try and be that way as well. It is just human nature to follow the lead of other people when they are doing things in the right manner and try to inspire others to behave in the same manner. Just like children mimic their parent's behavior, actions, mannerisms and values, so do employees mimic their manager to a certain degree. A good manager realizes this, understands why, and makes a solid effort to create a proper role model image for their employees.

Grow Your Employees

One important aspect of a manager's job is to provide guidance and support for their employees and to help groom them for higher or better positions within the company. While this might seem like the employee's responsibility, that manager's role in the growth of employee's careers should not be discounted.

One thing a great manager has is a great team or staff underneath them. These are people who perform well in their job, work well with others and people who know how things should go and how to complete a project or assignment within a stated deadline. These people are good at what they do and it takes a long time to build such a team and support structure.

But even though the manager wants and needs these people to stay in their roles in order to keep things moving smoothly, that is a very selfish attitude to take when it comes to individual employees. The manager should always do their part to see that qualified people advance within the organization at every opportunity.

Most employees have their eyes set on their career and what the next step should or might be. They also have a time frame in mind for when that next step should occur. If that time frame goes by and people are still in the same position, then boredom and frustration start to creep into their heads. When this occurs the chances of losing that employee increase greatly.

I knew a manager at one company who was afraid of losing valued and trusted employees because they made his life easier. So every time a promotion or better position came around he would block his employees from taking those jobs so he could keep his team intact. While this helped the manager, it hurt the employees and their attitude towards the company and the manager began to sour. It was only after losing a few employees to other companies that he began to see the error in his approach.

Great managers take an interest in every employee and work towards both preparing them for the next step in their careers and making them aware of opportunities as they become available. They will also mentor them as far as letting them know what they need to do in order to become qualified for that next step.

Most managers have at least one evaluation meeting with each employee every year and career advancement should become part of that meeting. This provides both employee and manager to sit down, discuss performance and also discuss where the employee wishes to go next in their career and how the manager can help them get there.

Together the manager and the employee create a plan that will help the employee get all the qualifications they need to qualify for the next level of employment while the manager tires to place the employee in the best position to get the real life experience and qualifications they might require as far as experience is concerned.

This might mean placing a certain employee in a project leadership position where they might get exposure to the people responsible for hiring certain people within the corporation. This way when positions do become available, the people hiring will already know the abilities and performance of the applicants. This is just one role the manager can play in helping their employees advance in their careers.

Managers who play an active and interested part of the employee's career growth usually enjoy a more positive relationship with the employees because they see the manager as someone who has a real and verified interest in making them success both as employees and as individuals. This inspires loyalty and a desire to perform at their highest level for someone they believe in and respect.

A more selfish role of the manager in advancing other employee's career is that a great manager always has a succession plan ready and waiting should the manager suddenly qualify for a new or higher position within the company.

When this happens the manager should have someone ready to take their position as manager and also have other people targeted to move up in the ranks as well. Finally, new employees are brought in to fill the lower positions and the process starts all over again.

Preparing employees for new and better roles is a very important part of any manager's responsibilities. This helps keep motivated employees moving in the right direction, improves performance and creativity, and helps strengthen the bond and relationship between manager and employee. Since that relationship is often the difference between success and failure for both the manager and employee, it just makes sense to take an interest in the future of each and every employee.

Be Fair

This is the first in a series of quick hitters that pertain to the personal characteristics of a great manager. These traits help form a good and positive perception as they pertain to the relationship between a manager and the employees.

Employees do not expect their manager to be their best friend or drinking buddy. But they do expect the manager be fair in their treatment of all employees. That means treating everyone the same way and not giving anyone preferential treatment unless there is a real and valid reason for it.

Employees do hot usually mind being given extra work or more responsibilities as long as they see other employees being asked or expected to do the same things. It is when they are being asked to do things differently, or when they are not receiving the same benefits or opportunities as others that problems start to surface.

As a manager, we must make a concerted effort to treat everyone the same way. While this is not often reasonable or possible, we must make an effort not to have "favorites" or people we have different levels of treatment for.

Not only are there business reasons for treating people all the same there are many legal reasons for this as well.

There are laws in place to protect employees from different levels of treatment from management within the company. You cannot, and should not, discriminate when it comes to how you treat and interact with all your employees. Performance and emotional issues aside, you could wind up on the wrong end of a lawsuit if you exhibit this type of behavior.

For example, you should not let some of your employees come in late or leave early on a regular basis while you dock other people's pay for doing the same thing. You should not ask one or two employees to always work weekends or evening when you never ask anyone else to do the same things. And you most definitely cannot give your personal friends the best assignments or preferential treatment because they are your friends.

While no one is perfect and no one situation is exactly like another, you should have specific reasons for any behavior or treatment that appears to be preferential. Be up front about it and take the time to explain certain things to your employees so they have a complete and accurate understanding of what has happened.

For example, if one of your employees asks you to leave early for the next week because their daughter is sick and has some hospital appointments for test, you can grant the request but you should let others know the reasons behind the perceived special treatment.

Or if your decision is based on a specific reasons, you should make that reason known and ask for their understanding.

A perfect example of this happened in a job I had many years ago where we were required to staff the office on holidays. My boss went to the staff and stated that he preferred to give Christmas off to the people who celebrated it so he would ask others to work that day while Jewish Holidays would be staffed by those who had to work on Christmas. Pretty much everyone appreciated the thought and concern that was behind that decision and no one complained about those assignments after that. Had the reason behind the assignments never been communicated, some people might have been resentful about working on Christmas.

Being fair also means being open minded when it came to disputes and issues within the office. Since the manager is often the first person people go to when it comes to disputes, it is important that the manager make an honest effort to understand the situation and make a fair and impartial decision or resolution.

Another important aspect of being fair to all employees is coming up next, That is:

Be Consistent

One thing employees find really frustrating is when the boss or manager tells them to do one thing today, something else totally different tomorrow and something in between the next day. All for the same or very similar situations. When the boss is all over the place with their instructions or guidance, employees have no idea what they should do the next time they are confronted with a similar situation.

Employees like managers and people who are consistent. This is because after a certain period of time they begin to understand how a person thinks and what they would like or expect to have happen in a certain situation. Then they know what to do and can get more resolved in less time than when they need to drop whatever they are doing and ask someone what they should do.

For example, let's say a customer purchased a product worth $50 and wanted to return it without a receipt.

The employee asks the manager and the manager replies that since they don't have a receipt then the product can be returned for a store credit only. So the employee issues a credit, the customer is happy, and everyone goes on with their day.

The next time a customer comes in with the same product without a receipt and wishes to return it the employee remembers the instructions they received last time and accepts the return with a store credit being given to the customer. Just like how the last customer was treated in the same situation. The result is that the matter was handled quickly and everyone was happy.

But suppose the manager goes to the employee and yells at them for accepting a return without a receipt? What might the employee do next time? The employee is now confused because they have received two different answers to the same situation or question and they have no idea which one to apply to the next time this happens. So the result is more waiting to get an approval or advice from someone who may or may not be readily available.

Consistency allows people to take on more control and know more of what should be done because they have been through the same situation before and this is what they were told. So they file that information aside and are ready to follow the same path.

This not only saves time for the customer and employee but also for the manager as well because they do not have to spend hours each day answering the same questions over and over again day after day.

Now we all realize that there might be different circumstances or exceptions to every rule and most employees understand this. But the manager who is the most consistent usually has employees who are among the most productive as well. That is because they can do more because they understand the manager's thought process and can connect the dots with this current situation.

I have always entrusted my employees to use their own judgment based on their past experiences and guidance from me. If they make a mistake, and they sometimes do, then we will discuss why that decision wasn't the right one and what should happen next time. As long as the employee had good reasons for what they did there is no problem.

All that being considered, it is also prudent for the manager to have safeguards in place to limit the exposure to the company for the cost of those mistakes. So I pick a dollar figure that I am comfortable with and let the employees know that as long as their resolution is less than a certain amount they can go ahead with what they feel is best. If it is over that dollar amount then they have to get pre-approval before making any commitments to the customers.

Being consistent also makes the employees feel more comfortable in their jobs and the actions they take within those jobs. Once they get a feel for what the managers likes and expects, they can go about following those guidelines. When the manager is all over the place in their thoughts, directions and actions, it makes it more difficult for everyone because no one knows what should be done in any situation.

Be Confident

Employees like to see confidence in their boss or manager. The look to them to give them a feeling of security and purpose when things might be going a little bad. More important, the manager is the one they look towards to provide stability and peace during stressful times. Are you a manager like that? Because if you are not, it is time to start creating a more confident self in the eyes of your employees.

Acting confident gives your employees the perception that all is well and that you are well in control of everything that is going on. Things can't be that bad because you do not appear worried. Nothing is really wrong because you don't appear upset. No challenge is too big because you appear to take everything in stride and have the confidence to handle anything that might come your way. As the captain of their ship, if you act safe your crew will feel safe as well.

Much of what a manager does is not fully understood by the employees.

While they understand that managers are accountable for certain things, they are not aware of all the pressures and responsibilities that the manager is up against every day. They are also not aware of certain facts or situations occurring at any given time.

Because there is a certain amount of unawareness they look at the manager for clues regarding how well or poorly things are going at that particular time or how good or bad a certain situation might. If the manager appears angry, upset or worried at that time, the employees might feel the same way as well.

Now that we understand this, we should also understand how the manager can go about instilling faith, confidence and calmness to their employees.

First of all, a great manager does not get overwhelmed very easily. They take things in stride and take the time to learn their jobs as best they can while learning also to anticipate things before they actually come around. This way they can become more prepared. That means being able to handle more things proactively and fewer things reactively.

When someone gets in over their head or allows themselves to become overwhelmed, it tends to make other people scared or overwhelmed as well.

But a great manager will take some time to look at the task at hand, or at the current situation, and instead of letting it consume them, they will break things down and come up with a manageable plan to tackle things head on.

A great manager has people who look up to them because they always appear in control with an action plan to handle anything they might come up against. This instills calm and purpose instead of panic and fright. In other words, if the manager isn't upset the employees are not likely to become upset either.

The second thing a good manager can do is become as good at their job as they possibly can be. Not at just the high level things but at the lower level things as well. They develop as complete a knowledge of how everything is done as possible. Even if they never have a reason to apply that actual knowledge they will learn it so they have a better and more complete overall knowledge than anyone else.

This includes the knowledge and development of a network of skills and contacts they can call upon to handle things as they arise. So often it is not so much knowing how to handle a certain task but who to turn to so it can be handled for you. So when things get really crazy, you can direct your employees to the right resources to help them get through what is ahead.

Possessing that knowledge will allow the manager to answer more questions, make better overall decisions and appear more confident and in control than the manager who only has a basic or high lever overview knowledge of what goes on. Confidence comes from knowing that you are the best resource available for certain information or guidance. When you feel confident you act confident.

The third thing great managers are able to do is have confidence in the people working for them. If a manager has faith and confidence in their staff then they can relax and respond confidently to any request or challenge. It is when the manager has little faith in their employees that problems arise that they get nervous.

Every manager need to develop faith and confidence in their employees. That kind of faith enables the manager to relax and behave more confidently because they realize that they have the people in place to handle almost anything. They realize they don't have to do everything. All the need to do is assign the right people to the right tasks and they are home free.

Fourth, and probably the most important thing, a great manager is able to hide his fears and emotions when needed. This is not dishonesty or deception but rather understanding that showing his or her fear is not the best way to proceed.

Therefore, the great manager understands the need to appear confident on the outside even though they are shaking in their shoes on the inside.

All of this is important because fear and panic negatively impact the attitude and performance levels of just about every employee. When people are scared or upset even the smallest task appear insurmountable and people tend to get more upset with every setback or roadblock the come in contact with. If left unchecked, fear and rumors can slowly bring things to a screeching halt in any office.

But when the leader appears strong and in control, others trend to feel the same way. They continue to perform with a purpose and a higher level of commitment. Employees look to their manager for security and guidance. When the person who delivers that guidance doesn't get overwhelmed or frustrated at anything, the employees usually don't get that way either.

Be Reliable

This one is a really easy one. Employees expect their managers to be reliable. That means being there when needed, stand behind your words and commitments and doing the things expected of you with regularity and commitment. It means showing your employees that you are just as committed to them as you want them to be committed to you.

Doing this is easy. Just follow a couple of easy steps:

Basically, if you are supposed to do something, just do it. Don't put it off and do it next week. If it is supposed to be done today, then do it today. Doing less than that sends the message that whatever it is that you are supposed to do is not considered all that important to you.

If there are deadlines that need to be met for any task, make sure you do your part to get everything done by that deadline.

For example, there is no reason an employee should go without a raise because you didn't get the paperwork submitted on time. Or, an employee should not miss out on a new job because you didn't submit their application until after the deadline.

If you say something, stand behind your words. If what you said turns out to be wrong, stand up and take the responsibility for what you said. No one expects or demands perfection but we do demand that people be responsible for what they say after they said it. Do not waffle, retract or change what you said or try to blame someone or something else. If you said something wrong, admit it, take responsibility and move on.

If you make a commitment to anyone, honor it. Your word should be your bond and you need to protect that bond by doing everything you possibly can to make sure you uphold your commitments. If, for some reason you find yourself unable to honor a commitment, give the other person or people an honest answer why you cannot do what you committed to. If you made a mistake and should not have made that commitment, just say that and ask for their understanding. Life is full of things that don't work out like we planned. We just have to do our part to the best of our ability.

If you are supposed to be somewhere by a certain time, be there a few minutes early. Showing up late sends the messages that other things were more important to you and that this had to wait.

Arriving late to a meeting or gathering is rude and condescending to everyone else who was there on time and is now having to wait for you.

If you are part of a team then be part of that team. Do not miss meetings, have too many other commitments or expect others to do your share of the work because you are too busy doing other things. Everyone on the team has others responsibilities as well and if they can do their part you should do your as well.

Last, but most certainly not least, if you make a mistake, own up to it, take the responsibility for that mistake and move on. Your primary focus must always be on how your employees perceive their manager. Owning up to your mistakes is better than to be seen running from them.

Be Aware

Having worked with several "clueless" bosses over the course of my life I can safely say that this one is one of the most important items on the list. Bosses that have no idea what goes on within their departments or staff can be dangerous when it comes time to make decisions or commitments. After all, one cannot possibly make an informed decision when they were not informed to begin with!

There are a lot of managers out there who feel that the day to day responsibilities and tasks performed by the employees are somehow beneath them. They sit in their offices handling the important stuff while the employees do the grunt work.

The problem is that this "grunt work" or every day activities are what produces the product, services and support functions that drive the company. While the individual tasks might be repetitive or seemingly unimportant, they all provide a vital function to make sure products are produced, bills are being sent out and customers are being supported.

These tasks represent the lifeblood of the company and manager's need to be aware of these tasks and what is involved in completing every one.

That is why sometimes the best managers are the ones who work their way up through the company and have an intimate knowledge of what is involved in doing certain functions. But sometimes people are brought in from the outside, given a manager's title and they sit behind their desks making decisions without really knowing what is involved in performing some of these functions.

I held a job once where I had no idea how long it took to do certain tasks or how much time was spent during any one week doing those tasks. It occurred to me that I need to understand this more fully understand these things before I could make decisions on workload and manpower and other things.

So I went to a person in each area and spent the morning with them just watching what they did and what was involved. I saw how long things took and I saw what I thought were certain inefficiencies and problems within the system as well. But what I really got from this exercise is a more thorough and complete understand of how long certain things took.

Very often upper management makes decisions based on what they think instead of what is reality. They might think something only takes 2 minutes when it might take 5 minutes or even 10 minutes. While this might seem like a little discrepancy, if you multiply that by the number of times that "little" task is done every day, the difference can be huge!

This does not mean that management is doing this on purpose. It just means that no one has actually spent the time to understand what is involved and how long something takes in real life. If the manager in charge of the people who did those things were present in the meeting and had spent the time to uncover this knowledge, he could have spoken about what really is happening and possibly changed some perceptions.

Another area where a great manager excels is in creating a great work environment. This requires being aware of what is going on in the office every day and taking steps to make the overall environment as positive and pleasing as possible. But many managers don't seem to feel that this is important enough to spend their time on.

Rumors, gossip and personality difference can cause massive problems within a crowded office. In a place where people usually must work closely together, having one or two people poisoning the working environment can negatively affect the entire office. The manager who walk in and shuts his door and distances him or herself from everything else can easily neglect the entire environment.

This means the manager must be aware of problems or troubles that are going on in and around the office. It means stepping in when needed to mediate a disagreement or deal with a workplace issue. These issues can range from complaints about the coffee machine in the break room to full blown sexual or physical harassment!

Left unaddressed means this type of behavior will continue to occur and the result is usually that the problem gets worse as more and more people are affected by it. There are some people who feel that if something is not addressed it is like the manager knows about it and is OK with it. Even though this is not likely the case, if the manager doesn't do anything about it then the problem is not going to go away by itself.

The entire point we are trying to make is that being a great manager is more than just assigning the right people to the right tasks and getting work done on time and with good results. It also includes caring for your employees and providing them with a good environment in which to do their work. This can only happen when the manager is aware of everything that is going on within the workplace and the tasks and jobs performed by their employees.

Be Specific

A great manager is someone who knows what they want or what needs to be done and is able to communicate that to their employees very clearly, accurately and specifically. In the workplace, being able to be specific about what is needed is one of the most important keys to getting more done in less time with less wasted time and resources.

Being specific helps reduce confusion and misunderstandings. It is far better to say "I need this to be 3 feet long" than to say "I need this to be a little bit longer. If the original object was 2 feet long then "a little bit longer" might be 25 inches, 27 inches or even 33 inches. All of those would fit the original request but none of them would be right.

Great managers avoid generalities whenever possible not because they mistrust their employees or do not believe they know how to do their jobs but because they understand that wrong results mean wasted time and usually wasted resources as well.

It is far better to be specific upfront than have to do something over later.

Employees usually like or prefer specific instructions because it gives them a clearly defined task that they can accomplish without being concerned as to whether they are doing the right thing or making the right choices. Any times you give someone a choice as to what to do you had better be prepared for the results.

Specific instructions also can reduce disagreements between employees working on a common project or task. The more specific the instructions the less likely disagreement will be as to how the team or group should proceed.

For example, let's say you need a report done by the end of the week. Your instructions are: "Please create a report for me on the Collins project. It should have a list of deadlines, financial reports to date, a list of people working on the project and their cell numbers as well as pictures taken of the progress. Do not put any profit figures in the report because it may be shown outside the company. It should be in Word Format and formatted in 8.5 X 11 format in landscape so the reports are more easily read. I need to report by 3PM Friday."

In your instructions you have made clear several things which will eliminate certain questions. For example, no one will ask you if you want pictures in the report because you said you do.

No one will ask if you if you want cell phone numbers included because you asked for them. Most important, no one will put profit figures in the report because you specifically said not to include them for obvious reasons. By giving a specific time and date at the end there is no confusion as to exactly when the report is due.

Great managers also realize that every question that might come up causes a delay in working on the project or at least pulls someone off of what they are doing in order to get the answer. By providing as much information as possible up front, you minimize questions, reduce wasted time and increase the chances of getting exactly what you want when you want it.

Great managers give some thought to their requests before making them and provide as much of the needed information as possible so that employees can do a better job in less time with far less stress and confusion. The result is that everything gets done faster, everyone has less stress and there is much less waste.

Be Focused

Great managers are those managers who are able to keep their minds on the tasks at hand while also being focused on what lies ahead as well. That means being able to manage several things at once without losing concentration or focus on anything. While that might seem like a tall order, it is much easier when you take some pretty easy steps that any manager can do.

First of all, great managers know the importance of focusing on what needs to be done to make sure things get done properly. When your attention is drifting between project and project or task to task, you not only lose time you lose concentration and train of thought.

Managers need to create an atmosphere where employees are allowed to focus as well. That means creating a work environment that is conducive to working and accomplishing objectives quickly and easily. That means removing distractions from the work environment during critical tasks.

Good managers also know how to lead by example and demonstrate to the rest of the employees how to stay focused and not allowing oneself to be distracted or brought off topic. This means showing employees how to begin a project and work through it to completion without wasted time, duplicated efforts and lost resources.

Managers are not allowed to "forget" to do important things or allow themselves to appear distracted or off track. Managers must lead by example and show others what can be accomplished when one is focused and in charge instead of distracted and disorganized.

Sometimes getting focused is as simple as removing distractions while other times a manager must devise some kind of process or system that allows him or her to keep several things going and instantly knowing where each project or task is going at any moment.

This may involve delegating responsibilities to other qualified people and letting them handle some of the manager's responsibilities. This will free up time for the manager to oversee several things at once and keep an eye over everything. Nothing says the manager has to do everything themselves but they are responsible for everything so delegation might be the way to go.

Other manager's rely on reports or written notes to remind them of where they left off or where a project is at that moment. This allows them to quickly bring themselves up to speed when the need arises.

This is another example of the manager not really needing to "know" everything but instead have access to information right when they need it.

Sometimes being focused means never losing sight of the "big picture" when working on smaller parts of it. Being able to remain focused on the overall objective when working on a much smaller aspect of it can help do things better and stay motivated. Not only that but knowing what the main objective helps you handle the smaller parts with greater accuracy and get much better overall results.

Great managers make their employees part of the big picture and constantly remind them of the importance of their individual efforts and roles in the entire project. People often get caught up in their own role and soon as no longer aware of why they are doing what they are doing. Great managers keep people focused on the big picture and constantly remind them of their role in it.

Great managers understand that they are human and that human's often make mistakes. So instead of relying on their memories or knowledge, they take steps to implement whatever external tools they have access to in order to help them become more focused on multiple things at the same time.

Focus is important when it comes to achieving both short-term and long-term goals. Managers and employees who are able to remain focused and deflect distractions are the people who accomplish much more in less time than their easily distracted counterparts.

Be a Team Player

This topic is an easy one for me to write because I have seen first-hand so many managers both succeed and fail strictly by the way they interact or "play" with others. Every manager with a staff that report to them work in a team culture or environment. By the definition of the word "team" that means everyone working together in order to achieve a common goal. It does not mean placing any one individual above the rest.

A great manager believes in working together and sharing the credit for work well done. The great manager understands that their success is the team's success as well. The manager should never take all the credit for the work of the team. Great managers understand this and make sure that efforts are recognized and rewarded.

At one job where I worked we had a manager who was good with his staff but whenever the staff did something good, the manager took all the credit.

Granted he spoke to the staff and told them what a great job they did which was nice, but he never gave anyone else credit for the work that was produced.

In one particular case, the manager took absolutely no part in a project whatsoever other than to let the employees know what had to be done. He gave no input during the course of the project, held no meetings or participating in any of the planning or work that was done on the project. But when the project was a success, there he was standing out in front willing to accept all the praise from upper management.

Behavior like this angers employees who worked hard only to see someone else step in and take credit for the work that they did. It also creates hard feelings and often results in lower productivity and poor attitudes within the employees.

Great managers understand that they are part of a team and that teams work together. Teams should equally share the rewards for work well done as well as the blame for when things go wrong. Really great managers will attempt to take some of the blame away from the team while letting most of the credit go to the team. Poor managers are quick to accept credit but always look for other to take the blame.

If you want to become a great manager, work with your team to achieve your goals. Retain the manager / employee relationship but work closely with employees without a big barrier between you and the employees. Instead of manager and employee become teammates.

Do not feel you are better than everyone else because you are the manager. Instead, think of ways that you can use your position as a manager to help the team with their goals. Work on ways to make the team more successful instead of just yourself. When you eliminate the barriers between you and the other team members, everything just flows better. More gets accomplished and more information is shared.

When it comes to your employees, great managers realize that as a manager, you are also the team leader and team leaders are also in charge of the welfare of the team members. This means watching out for members of the team and doing things to help each team member get the credit and recognition they need. It means developing team members so they become more and more capable of handling more and larger responsibilities. It means preparing team members for both the present and the future at the same time.

The success of the manager is closely tied to the overall success of those in his charge. If the team is successful, the manager will be successful. If the team is not successful, usually the manager will not be successful either. It makes sense for the manager to create a team culture and to become an integral part of that team and not just a figure head.

Be Respectful

This is one of these topics that should be included in any topic that involves interacting or working with others. Whether we are talking about the working environment or going out with friends or how we treat our spouse and children, there always should be one constant. We should always treat others with dignity and respect. If we are unable to do that we cannot expect others to treat us properly or respond to our requests or commands.

Managers need to be respectful of their employees because employees are people first and employees second. You cannot, and should not, expect any employee to leave their feelings and emotions at the door when they come to work. People are just not capable of doing that no matter how hard they might try.

Think about how you respond to other people who treat you poorly, talk down to you or treat you like you were less than the person you really are. Do you strive to prove them wrong and do better? Or are you resentful and either distance yourself from those individuals or fail to respond to whatever they want.

While some people will try to prove people wrong, most people will have a negative reaction to poor behavior on the part of another person. Even when the reaction is to show the other person they are wrong, it is usually in a way that will make the other person regret doing or saying what they did to the person in the first place.

For example, if the manager says they are poor performers and worthless, the employee might get more education, improve their skills and become more valuable an employee. Then, at the first chance, they will get a better job and leave without giving notice to show the boss they were wrong!

It has long been established that people respond better to positive comments and reinforcement than they do to negative comments or behavior. People genuinely try harder for people they respect or think highly of. That is just one of the values of having good relationships with your employees.

This does not mean that a manager can never say a bad thing about an employee. Sometimes, when an employee is performing at a lower than acceptable level, something needs to be said. But those conversations can take place in such a manner that the manager and employee are treated respectfully and with dignity.

You don't have to yell in order to get a point across. Most of the time all you need to do is inform the other person and show them the right way to do something next time.

Here are some things managers should always do when other people are involved:

First, never gossip or talk about other people behind their backs. Employees will think if you talk about other people behind their back to them, then you are probably also talking about them behind their backs. Even if this is not true the logic does often make a lot of sense.

Second, never make fun or talk badly about other people. It isn't nice to do that and it reflects badly on you as well. If you can't say something nice about someone else it is far better to say nothing at all. If others are saying bad things about someone else, it doesn't mean you have to join in. Take the high road and keep out of it. Words can come back to haunt you.

Third, if you have to discipline someone, do it in private and do it in a non-confrontational way and use the conversation as a teaching tool where the employee is told their weaknesses but also given a way to get improvement as well. This way both the employee and manager will benefit from the experience.

Fourth, avoid rough, crude or vile language. It offend many people and it reflects poorly on you as well. Keep comments respectful and do not sink to the other person's level even though you are provoked. Every confrontational needs someone to take the high ground and it should be you.

Fifth, religion, politics, race and sex have no business in a workplace conversation. This is especially true when it comes to manager and employee. Say the wrong thing, make the wrong reference or mention something improper and you can find yourself on the wrong end of a harassment complaint.

Sixth, refrain from certain off-color jokes, stories or comments. These easily offend some people and are inappropriate in the workplace. Resist the temptation to be "one of the boys" and keep your mouth shut.

Seventh, refrain from making negative comments about upper management or the direction of the company. Not only are these inappropriate, they might find their way back to those people you don't want to hear them.

Eighth, be on your guard 24 hours a day, 7 days a week. With everyone having a smart phone these days there is always the chance that your comments will be recorded, your actions recorded on video and both immediately uploaded to the internet for all the world to see. There is no such thing as privacy these days and you had best accept that and take the appropriate precautions.

There is an old saying that goes something like "If you wouldn't feel comfortable saying or doing something in front of your grandparents, then it is best not to say or do it in front of anyone else either. That just means if you are not comfortable doing something in front of anyone, you shouldn't do it at all.

The other aspect of this is something we have referred to several times already and that is that the manager is held to a higher standard than the employee. Employees look to the manager for guidance on what is right or wrong and acceptable versus unacceptable. If they see the manager telling off-color jokes, they will think that is OK for them to do. If they see the manager ridiculing or making fun of someone else, they will feel that is OK as well. It can be a slippery slope from that point on.

One last thing when it comes to being respectful as a manager. Being respectful also means interceding whenever you notice in appropriate behavior or comments being made in the workplace. Whether they are directed at one person or an entire group, those comments can hurt people or make them uncomfortable. As a manager you need to put an end to those comments and come to the defense of the people they are aimed at.

There is far too much bullying in this world and we should all take a stand to stop it and stop it now. Everything starts with treating others with dignity and respect.

If everyone would just do that bullying would vanish, workplaces would become less stressful and we could spend more of our time doing more positive and rewarding things instead of demeaning other human beings.

Be Organized

Every manager needs to be organized. There are just too many responsibilities for one person to keep track of without some organizational skills and system. There are a lot of managers in this world and some are well organized while others have trouble finding their shoes in the morning. Organization is required on several levels when you become a manager.

First of all, great managers know how to organize their lives, schedules, tasks and responsibilities. They have a system or a plan that enables them at a glance to know what needs to be done now, later or further in the future. Their "system" also makes it easy to see at a glance what is happening in the days ahead.

There is no one perfect system because everyone is different and everyone responds to different things in different ways. But despite this, it is almost universally agreed that a system where entries are written or typed in so that they can be easily stored, accessed and sorted is always the best.

Second, a great manager understands that all tasks and responsibilities are not created equal and that some are always going to be more important or urgent than others. Therefore, it is not as simple as a "first come, first served" system. Some things that come in today might be more important than something that came in last week. So it makes sense that whatever system we use must have the ability to allow us to prioritize what needs to be done or acted upon so we do the more important or critical items first and then move on to those not as pressing.

Poor managers allows tasks to control their time while great managers control when and how tasks are completed. By being pro-active and making sure everything gets done on their schedule and at their convenience, more gets accomplished in less time with much better results.

Most managers also have more than one project or responsibility going on at the same time and that requires careful coordination to make sure everything is done when it needs to be done. Since every task or project has multiple steps, and since future steps require certain things be done before the next step is started, this coordination is critical.

I have always found that having a list of things that need to be done makes handling all my responsibilities easier and more efficient.

In fact, I have used multiple lists to insure that I am always on top of things. Here is a rough summary of how a great manager organizes his tasks and responsibilities:

I have 4 basic lists. These 4 lists encompass everything I need to do over both long and short term.

The first is a listing of everything that I need to do along with the deadlines for each item. This is a very high level listing that lets me see at a moment's glance what needs to be done and when it need to be completed by. This list comes in handy when a new request is made because I can see what else is due or going on at that particular time and it helps me make the proper commitments.

The second list is my monthly list. It shows me everything that needs to be done during the current month. I find that this list helps me focus a little more on what is need to be completed over the next few weeks and helps me build my weekly list much easier and with more accuracy.

The third list is my weekly list which tells me what has to be done this week. I update the list every Friday morning so I can adjust the next week's list based on what has already been completed and for any new tasks that may come in at the last minute. I find it more useful to create this list on the Friday before so I know how to hit the ground running come Monday morning.

Another benefit of creating the list on Friday is that you are already in the flow of the previous week and you mind is still in "business mode".

While still in this train of thought you can schedule out the next week's tasks and this will enable you to quickly read your list on Monday morning and not have to worry about where you left off and how you should start the new week. Instead, you just look at the list and you are ready to get started without worry or waiting time trying to think about where you left off on Friday.

The fourth and last list are my daily lists. These lists, created from my weekly lists, break down the weekly tasks into easy to manage daily tasks. The tasks are also listed in the order they need to be completed in so that step 1 is always done before step 2 and etc. This alone makes life much easier and avoids wasted time and efforts by doing things in the right order.

I create each days list by spreading out equally all the weekly responsibilities. This helps me avoid last minute scrambles when something comes up or when I take longer than anticipated to do any one task. I always leave empty time on each daily list for daily jobs and things that pop up in the last minute. I try to fill up half the day with scheduled tasks and leave the other half open. You can always start the next day's tasks if you finish early and stay on track but you cannot easily create more hours in the day if you fall behind.

These lists are just guidelines to help me stay focused and in control. With several things going on at the same time it is easy to forget something until the last minute and then you need to scramble to get things done. When this happens quality usually suffers because you just don't have the time to do anything.

I should also mention that these lists work only as well as the effort used in creating and following them. The lists are not designed to do the work for you. There sole purpose is to remind you of what needs to be done and organize the process for you.

The other part of organization is how you file things or organize your office. If you are always wasting time looking for things because you don't know where you put them, you will always fall behind and will be constantly struggling to keep up. Having everything where it should be and knowing where and how to find things when you need them is an extremely important skill for any manager.

Another part of organization is keeping track of which employee is supposed to be doing which task and making sure that they are on track. This means setting up weekly or sometimes daily meeting to make sure every project or task is on track to be completed on or before the deadline. Of course, these weekly meeting should be on your weekly and daily lists so you have set aside the time required for those meetings.

If all of this sounds like a lot of work, it really isn't. In fact, by following a certain system that works for you, the time you spend operating the system will be saved several times over by being able to be more in control of your overall workload. It might take you an hour to create and maintain these lists or whatever system you have chosen, but it will save you several hours each week and help insure that everything gets done.

Great managers do NOT rely on their brains to remember every little deadline and detail of every task. They commit things to paper so that nothing is forgotten and nothing is lost. Plus, if they should get sick or otherwise not be available, someone can look at the lists and see what needs to be done and when it has to be completed by. Being organized is one of the most common parts of management that help separate the great managers from the poor ones.

Be Reasonable

Good managers are reasonable managers. Great managers look at what they expect to make sure it is reasonable and achievable before they make the request or assign the task. Another way of stating this is that great managers never intentionally set up their employees to fail. They have reasonable and real world expectations.

Some managers I have worked with would think nothing of telling their employees that they have 20 minutes to complete a task that should take 2 hours. They want what they want and don't think about whether or not their demands could actually be met. This results in frustration and anger from the employees.

A while back we talked about the need for the manager to have an understanding about what actually goes in every day in their department. We talked about how they should know how long certain tasks take and what is entailed in actually performing those tasks. This knowledge becomes even more critical when you are expecting someone to do something for you.

I have always believed that the best managers are the ones who push their employees to do better when they believed that was possible. But at the same time, keeping their assignments and demands within a reasonable level. If you honestly think a 20 minute task can be done in 15 minutes, then give it a try. But if you are proven wrong, do not continue to make that demand in the future.

Progress usually involves pushing people to do something better, faster, cheaper or smaller. There is no reason why managers should not push their employees to achieve better results. But the difference between great managers and poor ones is that the great ones know reasonable limits while the bad managers don't really care.

Most employees do not like to be pushed but the manager's role is not focused on being liked but instead on getting results. Employees usually do not like to be asked to something faster or more often because they feel like they are being pushed too hard. But once the find that they can do something better or faster they are usually receptive and feel good about themselves in the process.

Raising expectations is how we fix flaws in the system, create better processes, and make overall much needed improvements. But it is through reasonable expectations and smaller steps that major improvement are realized.

The key to making things better is to create an environment that encourages constant improving while keeping everything in the proper perspective.

No more is this necessary than when goals are created and assigned. If you remember from our chapter on goals, good goals that encourage and challenge people are those goals that are reasonable and achievable. We might ask our employees to attempt the difficult but we should not expect them to achieve the impossible.

Over the years I have seen and experienced several managers who demanded the impossible for no other reason than to keep their employees on their toes and to make sure he had "ammunition" to keep pay raises and promotions to a minimum. He thought he was being clever but the employee's soon saw through all of that and became angry. Most of the good employees left to work for other companies and his company eventually went out of business.

A coincidence? I really don't think so.

Be Able to Resolve Conflict

Managers are called to manage several people all working in the same environment. Whenever you have different personalities working side by side, there are bound to be disagreements and conflict. It is not reasonable to expect people to work out their conflicts all of the time and when people cannot resolve issues on their own, the manager must be able to step in and diffuse the situation and resolve the problem.

Even the most pleasant office will have its share of problems and disagreements. In many ways this is a healthy atmosphere because from disagreements come discussions and from discussion come new ideas, different thought process and sometimes even change. It is when disagreements become negative factors that problems occur.

In an office environment usually disagreements come because one or more people might be interested in themselves more than the office and put themselves above everything else. They take credit for work done by others, spread rumors behind the scenes and do everything they can to get credit at the expense of everyone else.

But sometimes disagreements might stem from how hot or cold the office is, which kind of music is played during the day and who is entitled to have next Friday off when two people want it. Then there are people who just have to have their way regardless of how trivial something might actually be.

Though the manager should let people work out their own problems whenever possible, there are times when office tension and problems affect the overall productivity of the office and its ability to provide quality work. When tensions interfere with the employee's ability to work together, then the manager has no choice but to step in and try to mediate a resolution.

Though the manager has the right and ability to dictate a resolution, great managers understand the need to work with the people involved to come to some kind of agreement or compromise that everyone is happy with. When the managers tells people how things are going to be, that does not guarantee that everyone will agree and accept that particular resolution.

So a great manager will have the skills necessary to first calm people down, get to the root of the matter and try to negotiate a possible resolution. He will make everyone a part of the discussion and listen carefully to all sides. At first he will make a recommendation and hope that everyone will agree with the proposal and be happy. But if people cannot agree, or refuse to negotiate, then the manager has no other option but to make a decision and then enforce that decision.

In listening to both sides the manager must not play favorites but at the same time they must be aware of what is legal and acceptable behavior. If any rules or laws are being broken, the manager must step in and stop the behavior from continuing. Then the manager should report the behavior to Human Resources so the proper procedures can take place. Failure to follow the correct procedures can result in criminal charge of fines.

But for every day office issues, a great manager let's people interact with each other and resolve their own issues whenever possible. But at the same time they keep their eyes and ears open for any signs of discontent and / or tension in the workplace. Sometimes the manager might put in place some kind of reporting process where employees can anonymously report any problems or issues within the office.

Regardless of how the manager is made aware of any situation or problem, once they are aware of it they need to take action or at least investigate the complaint or behavior. That means asking some questions, playing better attention or just evaluating the complaint to see if it has merit. After all, just because someone makes a complaint does not mean it is a legitimate issue.

Managing any group of employees can be a real challenge for any manager. But as long as the manager is engaged in how the office is running and take swift and appropriate action, they will usually be able to handle most issues and problems as they occur. It is when the manager turns a deaf ear to things when problems get bigger and harder to resolve.

So be fair, get all the facts and then do not be afraid to take appropriate action.

Be Human

We have already said more than a few times throughout this book that employees are humans first and employees second. What we mean by that is that employees are people just like you and I and they have the same needs and desires that we have. Failure to take this into consideration can make a manager appear cold hearted and more concerned with profit and loss than they are with the employees.

Businesses of all shapes and sizes have rules and regulations that determine how the business is run and how people are treated. Generally the larger the business the more rules and regulations there are and the thicker the employee manual will be. This is not done to make life more difficult or to be mean or cold hearted. It is done because it has to be that way in order to make certain that everyone is treated equally and fairly.

But a great manager understands that sometimes human needs and situations sometimes require special action and consideration. That might mean bending the rules or accommodating an employee in times of need. This might mean changing an employee's hours to make his or her commute a little bit easier or to allow them to attend to special family needs and events.

Though the manager should be thoughtful and accommodating, they also have to balance the needs of the employees with the requirements of the business at the same time. This might require asking other people to temporarily shoulder more of the workload or make other concessions to help out a fellow employee.

All we are saying is that employees appreciate a boss or manager who is aware that people have personal and family lives that sometimes require their presence and attention. They also appreciate a manager who has compassion for other people and tries to help out whenever it is needed. Employees who feel that way also usually have a better feeling towards their bosses and the company they work for. This almost always results in better efforts and higher productivity.

Of course, the opposite is also true. When employees work for someone who is totally "by the book" and shows no compassion or feelings towards an employee in need, the employees tend to think negatively towards both the manager and the company even though the company might not be at fault.

I have worked with some managers who did not care one bit about anything outside of work. They dedicated all their time to their jobs, neglected their families, and expected their employees to do the same. This did not work out well for either the manager or the employees.

So if you want to be a great manager, develop some compassion and understand that your employees have life outside of work. Also understand that one's personal problems can, and usually do, impact their work life as well so anything a manager can do to help an employee deal with those problems will help not only the employee but the manager and the company as well.

Oh, No!

That was 26 Ways & We Still
Have More to Talk About!

How About Some
Bonus Content!

Just Turn the Page
For Some More Great
Information & Advice!

Be Honest

Employees need to trust in their manager in order to be loyal and productive. They must believe them when the manager tells them something and they must believe the manager when they make a statement or a promise. The moment the employees cease to trust their manager the relationship between manager and employee starts to disintegrate.

Trust is something that takes a long time to establish and only second to destroy. Trust is built up over a period of time and over several incidents and situations. Only after a person demonstrates that they can be trusted will people actually trust them.

Unfortunately for most of us, the time when we gave others the benefit of the doubt is long over. We cannot afford to give people the benefit of the doubt anymore because when we do, the consequences can be huge. Theft, deceit, and scams permeate our culture today and trust is something that is harder to earn but valued even higher than before.

A manager is only as good as his word. If the manager lies about something or is dishonest in dealing with anyone, no one will trust him or her anymore. From that point on everything will be viewed with suspicion and it will become more and more difficult to get employees to stand behind you.

Fortunately for us, being honest is a relatively easy and straight forward process. All we have to do is tell the truth, don't take credit for things we didn't do, don't blame others for our mistakes and do what you said you would do when you said you would do it. There is nothing difficult or hard to understand when it comes to honesty.

Yet it is one characteristic of management that escapes many managers today. Don't be one of those managers. Be someone who can be trusted and relied upon to do the right thing even though it might not be the popular thing to do.

Be Protective

A great manager has the back of each and every employee. They look after every employee, take an interest in their careers and help them grow within the organization. They make sure the employees get credit for the things they do and they rarely miss a chance to give credit to those who do a good job.

If a promotion is available, they fight for a deserving employee to get that promotion. If an employee is having trouble at home, the manager will try and help them through it and do what he or she can do to make the process easier.

If there are problems in the workplace and someone is being treated unfairly or illegally, the manager will stand up and fight for that employee even when it might not be the easiest thing to do. In other words, the manager should be seen as an ally and not someone out for just themselves.

Last, but certainly not least, the manager should be someone that employees want to come to whenever they need help or guidance or have a problem. Life is more than just work and a great manager understands that and helps his or her employees through life as well as work.

Be an Isolationist

A great manager is someone who does his or her best to shield their employees from the day to day BS or nonsense that comes with the job. There is so much going on within any company and some employees have little or no control over such things. Yet they were burdened with them every day by constantly hearing about those things and more.

A good manager shares information they feel the employees should be aware of while shielding them from the day to day stuff that doesn't directly involve or concern them. Employees do not have to be concerned with every little e-mail or memo that appears in your inbox. They do not need to be informed of petty in-fighting or disagreements that cause problems within management.

A great manager shares the information that the employees need to hear or should hear and blocks all the rest. This allows the employees to function better, worry less and have an overall better attitude towards the company. The end result is a happier and less stressed out employee who will perform at a much higher level.

So the next time something comes down from above, ask yourself if the employees really need to know about whatever it is. If they do need to hear it, then share it with a positive spin and appear in control of the entire situation. But if they don't need to hear about it, or if it doesn't concern them, then consider shielding them from it.

You and your employees will be happier for it.

Conclusion

Being a manager is not as easy as it looks or appears. Only after you become a manager do you realize all that it involves and how hard it can be. But a good manager understands that their life, and job, can be made much easier by creating good relationships with their employees and by creating and building a good workforce.

The fact is, for years I was a manager in the busiest territory in the United States and I worked less than managers in far smaller and low volume territories. I didn't work less because I was lazy and my performance was always at or near the top of the company. The reason I had it easier than most other managers in the company is that I had a great group of people working for me.

These were highly skilled people who worked hard and achieved great results. But it was hard work at the beginning building this workforce.

It required replacing certain people, bringing in new people and training them and it required taking the time and making the effort to make sure these people were set up to succeed.

My turnover rate was way lower than any other area and most of the people working for me had over 10 years of experience. In fact, most of those people had more experience than I did. But we worked together very well, I always looked out for them and I took an interest in their careers and lives both business and personal.

These relationships that I have built over the years, using the same approach and techniques mentioned in this book, have served me very well. They have enabled me to accomplish far more in less time than my other counterparts and also without a lot of the nonsense that other managers constantly put up with.

I truly believe that a manager is only as good as the people who work for him and the manager is responsible for the employee / manager relationship. While my counterparts are working longer and harder, I just let my team work like they are accustomed to and we always come out on top.

Not because I am the best manager in the whole world but because everyone believes in each other, appreciates everything we all do for each other and honestly wants each other to succeed both in life and in business. In short, we all do what is needed to make life easier.

No matter what industry you work in or how many employees you are responsible for, the chief idea remains the same. That idea is to develop your employees for the future, manage them equally and fairly today and make sure they have what it takes to do their jobs as efficiently as they properly can. Be a resource for them and make sure you are available to them when they need you.

Most important, do not set yourself aside from them. Do not act or behave like you are better than they are or place yourself on another level. Retain the distinction between employee and manager but do not treat them as inferiors in any way. Show your employees respect and compassion and they will reward you with higher efforts, more productivity and better overall performance.

All because you, as their manager, understand that employees are people first and as people they have the same needs and desires as you and I have. And we manage them accordingly. It's not all that hard and the rewards are amazing.

www.ingramcontent.com/pod-product-compliance
Lightning Source LLC
Chambersburg PA
CBHW051715170526
45167CB00002B/670